Contents

Senses

We all have five senses.

The Five Senses

ing

Rissman

ree

www.raintreepublishers.co.uk

Visit our website to find out more information about Raintree books.

To order:

☎ Phone 0845 6044371

▤ Fax +44 (0) 1865 312263

▤ Email myorders@raintreepublishers.co.uk

Customers from outside the UK please telephone +44 1865 312262

Raintree is an imprint of Capstone Global Library Limited, a company incorporated in England and Wales having its registered office at 7 Pilgrim Street, London EC4V 6LB – Registered company number: 6695582

Text © Capstone Global Library Limited 2010
First published in hardback in 2010
Paperback edition first published in 2011
The moral rights of the proprietor have been asserted.

Edited by Rebecca Rissman and Catherine Veitch
Designed by Ryan Frieson and Kimberly R. Miracle
Original illustrations © Capstone Global Library
Illustrated by Tony Wilson (pp. 10, 22, 23)
Picture research by Tracy Cummins
Originated by Capstone Global Library
Printed in China by South China Printing Company Ltd

ISBN 978 0 431 19478 3 (hardback)
14 13 12 11 10
10 9 8 7 6 5 4 3 2 1

ISBN 978 0 431 19484 4 (paperback)
15 14 13 12 11
10 9 8 7 6 5 4 3 2 1

British Library Cataloguing in Publication Data
Rissman, Rebecca
Seeing (The Five Senses)
612.8'4--dc22
A full catalogue record for this book is available from the British Library.

Acknowledgments
The author and publishers are grateful to the following for permission to reproduce copyright material: Age Fotostock pp. 17 (© Mirek Weichsel), **23 D** (© Mirek Weichsel); Corbis p. 19 (© karan kapoor/Cultura); Getty Images pp. 8 (Jonathan Kirn), 11 (Bob Elsdale), 20 (Michael Denora), 21 (altrendo images); Photolibrary pp. 4 (Polka Dot Images), 5 (LWA/Dann Tardif), 13 (Imagesource Imagesource), 16 (Aurelie and Morgan Da); Shutterstock pp. 6 (© Katarzyna Mazurowska), 7 (© Monkey Business Images), 9 (© Kristian Sekulic), 12 (© Losevsky Pavel), 14 (© Jacek Chabraszewski), 15 (© Ben Heys), 18 (© David Lade), **23 A** (© Kristian Sekulic), **23 C** (© David Lade).

Cover photograph of a girl making a frame with her fingers reproduced with permission of Photolibrary (Fancy). Back cover photograph of a close-up of a woman's eyes reproduced with permission of Shutterstock (© Kristian Sekulic).

The publishers would like to thank Nancy Harris, Yael Biederman, and Matt Siegel for their assistance in the preparation of this book.

Every effort has been made to contact copyright holders of any material reproduced in this book. Any omissions will be rectified in subsequent printings if notice is given to the publisher.

We use our senses every day.

Seeing and touching are senses.

Tasting, smelling, and hearing are also senses.

How do you see?

eye

You use your eyes to see.

Your eyes are in your head.

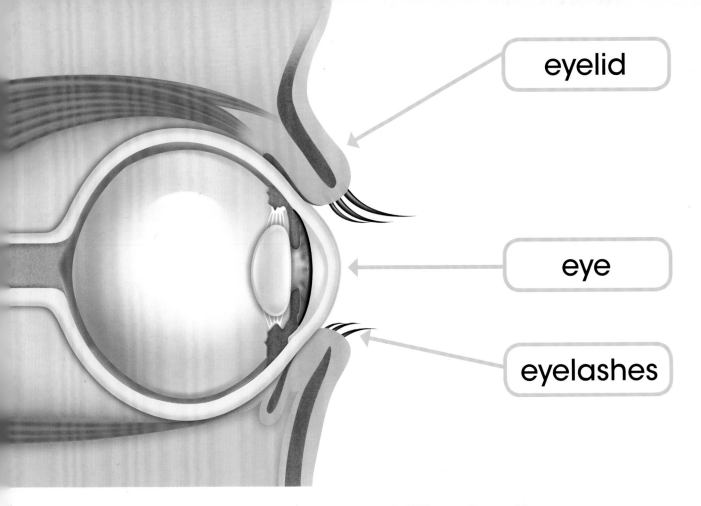

eyelid

eye

eyelashes

Your eyes are round like balls.
Your eyes have many parts.

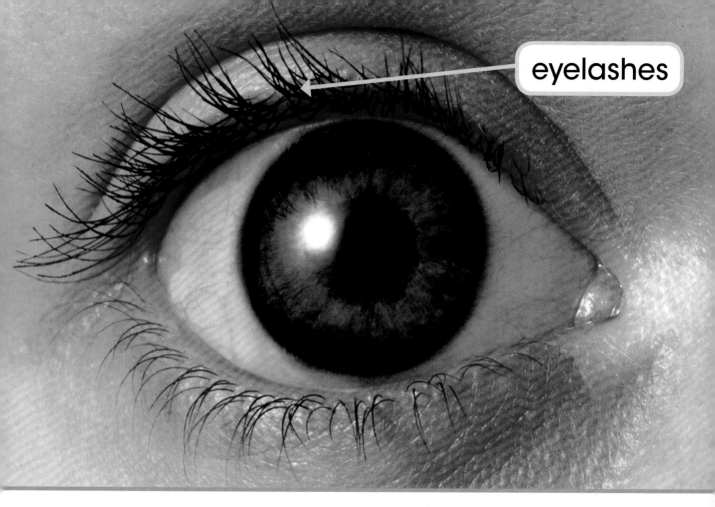

eyelashes

Your eyelashes help keep dirt out of your eyes.

What can you see?

Your eyes can see colour.

Your eyes can see shapes.

Your eyes can see things that are near.

Your eyes can see things that are
far away.

Your eyes can see big things.

Your eyes can see small things.

Protecting your eyes

Sunglasses can protect your eyes.

eyelid

Your eyelids can protect your eyes.

Helping people see

glasses

Some people wear glasses to help them see.

Some people do not see at all.
They use other senses to help them.

Naming the parts of the eye

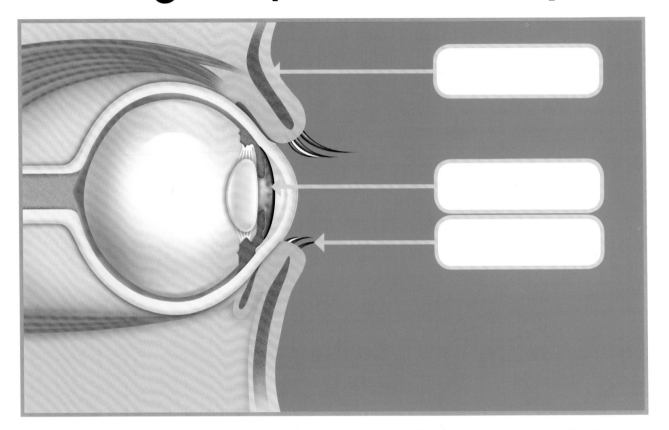

Point to where these labels should go.

eyelid   eye   eyelashes

Answer on page 10.

Picture glossary

eyelashes small hairs on your eyelids that help keep dirt out of your eye

eyelid part that covers and protects your eye

protect keep something or someone safe

sense something that helps you smell, see, touch, taste, or hear things around you

Index

Note to parents and teachers

Before reading

Explain to children that people use five senses to understand the world: seeing, hearing, tasting, touching, and smelling. Tell children that there are different body parts associated with each sense. Then ask children which body parts they think they use to see. Tell children that they use their eyes to see.

After reading

• Show children the diagram of the eye on page 22. Ask them to point to where the labels "eyelid," "eyelashes," and "eye" should go.

• Explain to children that some people are visually impaired. These people may wear glasses to help them see. Explain that some visually impaired people use other senses such as touch. They may use a cane to get around, and read Braille. Find an example of Braille text and encourage children to feel the bumps.